HORNS, HUMPS, and HOOKS

Lynn M. Stone

Rourke

Publishing LLC

Vero Beach, Florida 32964

www.rourkepublishing.com

PHOTO CREDITS: © Lynn Stone: title page, 4, 5, 7, 9, 11, 13, 15, 16, 17, 18, 19, 20, 21; © www.davehuss.com: page 6; © Paulo Ferreira: page 8; © Todd Smith: page 10; © Stephen Inglis: page 12; © Eliza Snow: page 14

Editor: Meg Greve

Cover design by: Nicola Stratford, bdpublishing.com

Interior design by: Renee Brady

Library of Congress Cataloging-in-Publication Data

Stone, Lynn M.

Horns, humps, and hooks / Lynn M. Stone.
     p. cm. -- (What animals wear)
  Includes index.
  ISBN 978-1-60472-309-0 (hardcover)
  ISBN 978-1-60472-787-6 (softcover)
 1. Horns--Juvenile literature. 2. Humps (Anatomy)--Juvenile literature. 3.
Claws--Juvenile literature. I. Title.
  QL942.S757 2008
  591.47--dc22
                          2008012969

Printed in the USA

CG/CG

Table of Contents

Horns

Bighorn sheep and a few other mammals have true horns. Horns are hard, like bone.

Bighorn sheep and other mammals with horns never shed them.

Horns grow from an animal's head. Horns take many shapes. An animal with horns does not shed them.

A bull has horns.

This elk has **antlers**. Animals with antlers like this elk, shed them each year.

7

Animals have horns for protection. The tips of horns are usually sharp.

The African Cape buffalo's horns help protect it from lions.

Animals use their horns to fight other animals. Fights decide which one is the toughest.

Males fight with their horns to win females.

Humps

Several kinds of big mammals have humps. A camel's hump, or humps, store fat, not water.

As many as 80 pounds (36 kilograms) of fat in a camel's hump help it to travel long distances.

Male bison, moose, and Brahma cattle also have large humps. The bison's hump is more muscle than fat.

A male moose has a hump and antlers.

A bull bison's hump muscle helps support its huge head.

15

Hooks

Some animals have features that look like hooks. **Birds of prey** have hooked toes called **talons**.

The bald eagle's talons are sharp and curved like fishing hooks.

Birds of **prey** have hooked beaks to snip, cut, and tear. Cats of all kinds have hooked **claws** to grab their prey.

Tigers scratch trees with their claws to mark their territory.

Horns, humps, and hooks may seem curious to us. However, they are very natural to the animals that have them. These special features help them survive.

A young bald eagle tears prey with its hooked beak.

Glossary

antlers (ANT-lurz): pointed bony growths on the skulls of deer and their cousins, which are shed each year

bighorn sheep (BIG-horn SHEEP): a type of North American wild sheep with large, curled horns that do not shed

birds of prey (BURDS UV PRAY): hunting birds with sharp beaks and talons such as eagles, hawks, and owls

 **claws** (KLAWZ): strong, curved nails on an animal's foot

 **prey** (PRAY): an animal that is hunted by another animal for food

 **talons** (TAL-unz): the sharp toes of certain birds

Index

Further Reading

Cooper, Jason. *Antlers and Horns.* Rourke, 2006.

Lark Books Staff. *Fangs, Claws, and Talons.* Sterling, 2007.

Ripple, William John. *Camels*. Capstone Press, 2006.

Websites

www.animals.nationalgeographic.com/animals/mammals/Bactrian-camel.html

www.teacher.scholastic.com/activities/explorations/bats/libraryarticle.asp?ItemID=239&Subjectl

www.kidsolr.com/science/page19.html

About the Author

Lynn M. Stone is a widely-published wildlife and domestic animal photographer and the author of more than 500 children's books. His book *Box Turtles* was chosen as an Outstanding Science Trade Book and Selectors' Choice for 2008 by the Science Committee of the National Science Teachers' Association and the Children's Book Council.